Grandma &
Grandpa -
Merry Christmas!
Love, Meghan & Tim

CHRISTMAS
STORIES

PUBLICATIONS INTERNATIONAL, LTD.

CHRISTMAS STORIES
TABLE OF CONTENTS

The First Christmas

Luke 2: 1–16   *Illustrated by Robin Moro*

And it came to pass in those days, that there went out a decree from Caesar Augustus, that all the world should be taxed.

(And this taxing was first made when Cyrenius was governor of Syria.)

And all went to be taxed, everyone into his own city.

And Joseph also went up from Galilee, out of the city of Nazareth, into Judea, unto the city of David, which is called Bethlehem; (because he was of the house and lineage of David):

To be taxed with Mary his espoused wife, being great with child.

And so it was that while they were there, the days were accomplished that she should be delivered.

And she brought forth her firstborn son, and wrapped him in swaddling clothes, and laid him in a manger; because there was no room for them at the inn.

And there were in the same country shepherds abiding in the field, keeping watch over their flock by night.

And lo, the angel of the Lord came upon them, and the glory of the Lord shone round about them: and they were sore afraid.

And the angel said unto them, Fear not: for, behold, I bring you good tidings of great joy, which shall be to all people.

For unto you is born this day in the city of David a Saviour, which is Christ the Lord.

And this shall be a sign unto you; Ye shall find the babe wrapped in swaddling clothes, lying in a manger.

And suddenly there was with the angel a multitude of the heavenly host praising God, and saying,

Glory to God in the highest, and on earth peace, good will toward men.

And it came to pass, as the angels were gone away from them into heaven, the shepherds said one to another, Let us now go even unto Bethlehem, and see this thing which is come to pass, which the Lord hath made known unto us.

And they came with haste, and found Mary and Joseph, and the babe, lying in a manger.

Silent Night

Fr. Joseph Mohr
Franz Gruber

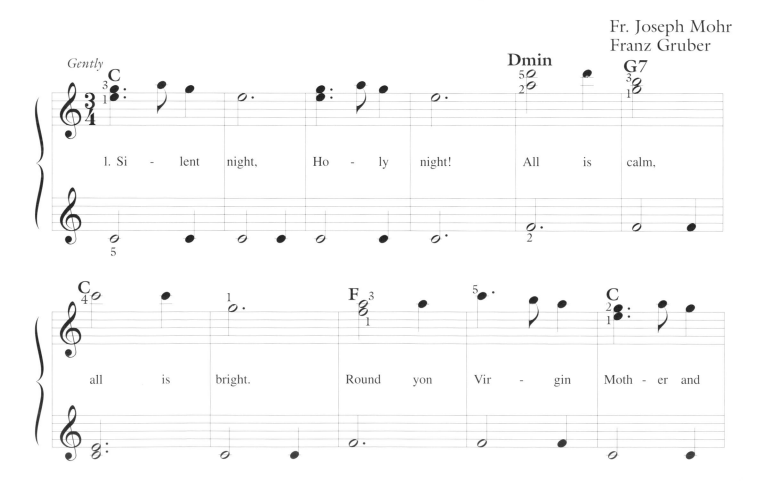

Gently

1. Si - lent night, Ho - ly night! All is calm,

all is bright. Round yon Vir - gin Moth - er and

2. Silent night, Holy night!
Shepherds quake at the sight.
Glories stream from heaven afar,
Heav'nly hosts sing Hallelujah,
Christ the Saviour is born,
Christ the Saviour is born.

3. Silent night, Holy night!
Son of God, love's pure light.
Radiant beams from Thy holy face,
With the dawn of redeeming grace,
Jesus Lord at Thy birth,
Jesus Lord at Thy birth.

A Visit From St. Nicholas

Written by Clement Clarke Moore   Illustrated by Tom Newsom

'Twas the night before Christmas, when all through the house,
  Not a creature was stirring, not even a mouse.
The stockings were hung by the chimney with care,
  In hopes that St. Nicholas soon would be there.

The children were nestled all snug in their beds,
  While visions of sugarplums danced in their heads.
And Mamma in her kerchief, and I in my cap,
  Had just settled down for a long winter's nap.

10

When out on the lawn there arose such a clatter,
    I sprang from the bed to see what was the matter.
Away to the window I flew like a flash,
    Tore open the shutter and threw up the sash.

The moon on the breast of the new-fallen snow
    Gave the lustre of midday to objects below.
When what to my wondering eyes should appear
    But a miniature sleigh and eight tiny reindeer.

With a little old driver, so lively and quick,
    I knew in a moment it must be St. Nick!
More rapid than eagles, his coursers they came,
    And he whistled, and shouted, and called them by name.

"Now, Dasher! Now, Dancer! Now, Prancer and Vixen!
    On, Comet! On, Cupid! On, Donner and Blitzen!
To the top of the porch, to the top of the wall,
    Now, dash away, dash away, dash away all!"

As dry leaves that before the wild hurricane fly,
    When they meet with an obstacle, mount to the sky,
So up to the housetop the coursers they flew,
    With the sleigh full of toys and St. Nicholas, too.

And then, in a twinkling, I heard on the roof,
  The prancing and pawing of each little hoof.
As I drew in my head, and was turning around,
  Down the chimney St. Nicholas came with a bound.

He was dressed all in fur, from his head to his foot,
  And his clothes were all tarnished with ashes and soot.
A bundle of toys he had flung on his back,
  And he looked like a peddler just opening his sack.

His eyes, how they twinkled, his dimples, how merry!
  His cheeks were like roses, his nose like a cherry.
    His droll little mouth was drawn up like a bow,
      And the beard of his chin was as
          white as the snow.

The stump of a pipe he held tight in his teeth,
 And the smoke, it encircled his head like a wreath.
He had a broad face and a little round belly,
 That shook when he laughed, like a bowlful of jelly.

He was chubby and plump, a right jolly old elf,
 And I laughed when I saw him, in spite of myself.
A wink of his eye, and a twist of his head,
 Soon gave me to know I had nothing to dread.

He spoke not a word, but went straight to his work,
 And filled all the stockings, then turned with a jerk.
And laying his finger aside of his nose,
 And giving a nod, up the chimney he rose.

He sprang to his sleigh, to his team gave a whistle,
 And away they all flew like the down of a thistle.
But I heard him exclaim, as they drove out of sight,
"Happy Christmas to all, and to all a good night!"

15

O Christmas Tree

Germany

Moderately

1. O Christ-mas tree, O Christ-mas tree, How love-ly are your branch-es,

So green and bright in sum-mer-time, As well as win - ter's snow-y clime, O

2. O Christmas tree, O Christmas tree,
   Much pleasure doth thou bring me.
   For every year the Christmas tree,
   Brings to us all both joy and glee.
   O Christmas tree, O Christmas tree,
   Much pleasure doth thou bring me.

3. O Christmas tree, O Christmas tree,
   Thy candles shine out brightly.
   Each bough doth hold its tiny light,
   That makes each toy to sparkle bright.
   O Christmas tree, O Christmas tree,
   Thy candles shine out brightly.

A Christmas Carol

Adapted by Lisa Harkrader   Illustrated by Diana Magnuson

Ebenezer Scrooge hunched over his account books. Scrooge's clerk, Bob Crachit, huddled at his own desk in the tiny outer office. The front door burst open, and a blast of December air whipped through the two rooms.

"Merry Christmas, Uncle!" said Scrooge's nephew.

"Christmas," muttered Scrooge. "Bah! Humbug!"

"You can't mean that, Uncle," said his nephew. "Why don't you close early today?"

"And become like other Christmas fools, buying gifts I can't afford?" Scrooge turned back to his books. "No thank you."

"Suit yourself," said his nephew. "But I hope you'll at least stop by for Christmas dinner tomorrow."

When his nephew opened the door to leave, another gust of wind burst into the office. With it came the sound of carolers singing. Scrooge banged his window open. "You!" he shouted at the carolers. "You there!"

One of the carolers, a young boy, stopped singing and stared up at Scrooge.

"How can a person do an honest day's work with you howling outside his office?" Scrooge snarled. "Find another street corner for your noise. Leave me in peace!"

Scrooge banged the window shut. "Merry Christmas indeed," he muttered. "What do they have to be merry about?"

"Sir?" Bob Crachit tapped on Scrooge's door. "I've copied all the letters and filed the paperwork. I also brought in more firewood and swept out the ashes. And, well, it's closing time, Mr. Scrooge."

"Fine," said Scrooge. "If your work is finished, you may leave."

"Mr. Scrooge?" said Crachit. "Tomorrow is Christmas, a day to spend with family."

"You'd like the day off, I suppose?" Scrooge said, as he glared at him.

18

"Well, yes, Mr. Scrooge," said Crachit. "After all, it *is* Christmas."

"Christmas? Bah!" Scrooge shook his head. "Fine. Take tomorrow off, but be here early the next day."

"Yes, sir. You can count on it, sir," Crachit said, as he pulled his coat snug around him. "Merry Christmas, Mr. Scrooge."

"Humbug," growled Scrooge. He opened the front door, and Crachit scurried out.

At the corner, neighborhood boys were sledding down a steep hill. Crachit leaped headlong onto one of the sleds and slid to the bottom of the hill, laughing and shouting, "Merry Christmas!"

"Fool," Scrooge scowled. He settled back into his chair and finished tallying his accounts.

Darkness fell, and Scrooge closed the last account book. He stood and stretched, his back stiff from the cold and the many long hours hunched over his work. It was time to go home.

As he locked the countinghouse, he glanced at the sign above the door. It read: THE FIRM OF SCROOGE AND MARLEY.

"Jacob Marley," said Scrooge. "A man who knew the value of a day's work. Too bad he's gone."

Scrooge trudged home, climbed the steps to his bedroom, and went to sleep. CLANK! "What was that?" Scrooge listened carefully, but heard nothing.

"I must have been dreaming," he muttered.

CLANK! CLANK! Scrooge sat up straight in his bed. "This can't be a dream," he whispered.

"No, it isn't a dream, Ebenezer." A voice echoed through Scrooge's bedroom.

A man, pale and ghostly, drifted into the room.

Scrooge stared at him. "Marley? Jacob Marley? How can that be? You're —"

"Dead." The ghost nodded. "And paying for my sins."

"Sins?" Scrooge frowned. "But you were a good man, Jacob. A fine businessman."

"Business? Hah!" Marley's ghost shivered. Business is meaningless. I never learned the value of love and charity. Now I wander the earth, unable to find peace."

"I don't understand, Jacob," Scrooge whispered.

"You must try to understand," the ghost said. "The same fate awaits you, Ebenezer, unless you change your ways. Three spirits will visit. The first will arrive when the clock strikes one."

The ghost silently vanished, and Scrooge pulled the covers over his head.

BONG! The clock struck one. "Ebenezer? Ebenezer Scrooge?"

Scrooge peeked out from beneath his sheets. A woman, pale and shimmering, stood beside his bed. In her hand she held a sprig of holly.

"Who are you?" whispered Scrooge.

"I am the Ghost of Christmas Past," said the ghost, as she motioned to the door. Scrooge crept from his bed and followed the ghost. The room began to dissolve, and soon he was staring into the window of another room, small and dark.

"This house," said Scrooge. "It seems familiar. Why, it's the house I grew up in."

"Yes." The ghost nodded. "And the boy? Is he familiar, too?"

Scrooge peered through the window. A small boy sat alone in the corner, reading a book. Scrooge's eyes grew wide. "It's me as a child! But why am I—why is he—sitting by himself?" Scrooge stared at the boy. "It's Christmas Day, isn't it?"

The ghost nodded, then asked, "And where are your parents?"

Scrooge frowned. "Working, I suppose. They worked to give me the things I needed."

"And did they?" asked the ghost. She motioned toward the boy. "Did they give you what you needed?"

Scrooge studied the boy. He looked well-fed and well-dressed, but his eyes were sad and scared. He reminded Scrooge of the young caroler from the night before. Scrooge then remembered how he had yelled and frightened the boy.

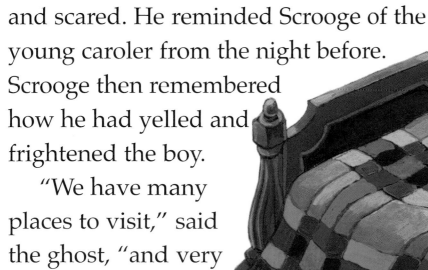
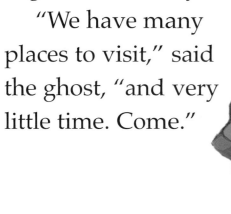

"We have many places to visit," said the ghost, "and very little time. Come."

The small, dark house faded away, and in its place stood a bright office filled with many workers. "I know this office!" said Scrooge. "I worked here. I was Mr. Fezziwig's apprentice. Look! There he is!"

Scrooge pointed to a man carrying a platter of roast beef into the office. Mrs. Fezziwig followed with a tray of pastries. Behind her came house servants carrying bread and pudding and mincemeat pies.

"Stop your work," Mr. Fezziwig told the office clerks. "It's Christmas Eve!"

A fiddler began playing, and Mr. Fezziwig led his wife to the center of the room. He took her in his arms, and they danced a lively jig around the office. The clerks clapped and tapped their feet, and several other couples joined the dance.

22

The Ghost of Christmas Past glanced at Scrooge. "This certainly isn't the firm of Scrooge and Marley, is it? Do you recognize the clerk in the corner?"

Scrooge stared at the young man. "Me," he whispered. "It's me."

The young Scrooge laughed and clapped to the music. His eyes were bright, his cheeks pink—so different from Scrooge's own clerk, Bob Crachit, who had huddled in the cold the night before, working quietly, his face pale and shadowed.

"I hope this party never ends," young Scrooge called out. "Let's stay and dance forever!"

Old Scrooge thought about Crachit, who had scurried away from the office as quickly as he could on Christmas Eve. "Crachit couldn't wait to get away from me," he said.

The music faded. Fezziwig's office dissolved into darkness.

"We have one more stop," said the ghost. "Our time is running out."

The ghost waved her arms, and Scrooge saw his younger self again, sitting in a garden beside a lovely young woman.

The woman's eyes filled with tears as she said, "I can't marry you, Ebenezer. There's something you love more than me."

"Nonsense," said the young Ebenezer.

The woman dabbed her eyes with her handkerchief. "You love money. You love it more than anything." The woman ran from the garden.

Old Scrooge and the ghost followed her. Scrooge could see she was now a few years older. She was in a parlor that had been decorated for Christmas. Children laughed and played at her feet. A little girl threw her arms around her and kissed her.

"You could have made her that happy," the ghost said quietly.

"Take me home!" Scrooge winced, "I can't bear it."

23

BONG! BONG! The clock struck two. Scrooge was back in his own bed.

"Thank goodness," he said, as he sank back onto his pillow. "It was a dream."

"No, Ebenezer. It wasn't a dream." A large man, glowing and transparent, stared down at Scrooge.

"I am the Ghost of Christmas Present," he said. "I have much to show you. Grab onto my robe." He clapped his hands. "Hurry! We cannot be late."

Scrooge touched the hem of the spirit's robe. The bedroom vanished, and Scrooge found himself on a busy, snowy street. The dark of night had disappeared, and now the morning sun peeked over holly-draped storefronts. Men and women bustled along the sidewalks, while their children laughed and skipped at their sides.

"Everyone looks so happy," grumbled Scrooge.

"Of course they do," said the ghost. "It's Christmas."

Scrooge shook his head. "You mean they all woke up happy, simply because the calendar said December 25?"

The ghost smiled. "Yes. Today they can forget their labors and their troubles, and simply enjoy their families, the fine food on their tables, and the blessings in their lives. When was the last time you stopped and enjoyed the moment, Ebenezer? Try it now. Close your eyes."

Scrooge frowned and closed his eyes. The aroma of freshly baked bread mingled in the crisp morning air. Horses clip-clopped over the cobblestone street. An icy snowflake tickled his tongue, and his mouth stretched into a wide smile.

The ghost led Scrooge down the street and into a tiny house. Beside a small Christmas tree, a man was playing with his children—three boys wearing patched trousers and two girls whose dresses were faded and frayed. The man looked up. He was Scrooge's clerk, Bob Crachit.

"Crachit!" Scrooge frowned at the threadbare furnishings. "This is where he lives?"

The ghost nodded. "It's all he can afford. His employer is a bit of a miser."

A woman, Mrs. Crachit, carried a small turkey into the dining room on a platter. She had adorned her dress with bright red ribbons, but her dress was mended and worn. She smiled as she carried the platter to the table.

The older children giggled and scrambled to the table.

"Their clothes are rags," said Scrooge, "and their turkey is nothing but bones."

Bob Crachit lifted the youngest boy from a chair in the corner and carried him to the table. The boy was pale and thin and carried a crutch. His name was Tiny Tim.

Tiny Tim raised his cup of water and smiled.

"Merry Christmas!" he said. "God bless us every one."

"What is wrong with that child?" Scrooge asked.

"Come," said the ghost, and he turned to leave.

"Wait," Scrooge said. "Their child is hurt, their turkey is all bones. Tell me why they are so happy."

BONG! BONG! BONG! Scrooge blinked. He was in his own bed again, and the Ghost of Christmas Present was gone. But as he sat up, another ghost floated into the room. He was draped in black, and a dark hood hid his face. Scrooge pulled the sheets to his chin. "Who are you?" he asked. The phantom said nothing.

"First came the Ghost of Christmas Past, then the Ghost of Christmas Present," Scrooge said as he stared at the phantom. "You must be the Ghost of Christmas Yet to Come?"

The phantom gestured toward the door. Scrooge followed him to the street in front of his countinghouse. The door was locked, and the windows were dark. Three men stood out front, talking and shaking their heads.

"I know those fellows," said Scrooge. "I do business with them. We are quite friendly. These men like me, even if my own nephew does not."

The ghost led Scrooge closer so he could hear what the men were saying.

"Poor old Scrooge," said one. "They say he's very sick."

"He must be near death if he's closed up his firm for the day," said another.

"If I know Ebenezer," said the third man, "he'll work during his own funeral."

The men laughed. "It is bad news, though," said the first man. "If Scrooge closes down, I'll have to find another countinghouse."

Scrooge turned to the ghost. "But I'm not closing down. Please, why did you bring me here?"

The phantom turned and drifted down the street. Scrooge followed him and soon found himself in a tiny room with faded walls and worn furnishings.

"But this is Crachit's house," Scrooge said as he peered around the room. "I've already seen them."

The spirit shook his head and led Scrooge into a bedroom that was hardly bigger than a closet. Mr. Crachit sat next to a small bed and held Tiny Tim's hand. Tears trickled down Mr. Crachit's cheeks.

"What's wrong with them?" asked Scrooge. "They were so happy last time I was here, laughing and playing. And where's Mrs. Crachit?"

The bedroom door opened, and Mrs. Crachit came in. Scrooge watched Tiny Tim sleeping in the bed. He was thinner than he had been at Christmas dinner, and his face was drawn and pale. His crutch rested against the bed, and a ball of mistletoe hung above his head.

"Did you see him?" asked Mrs. Crachit. "Will the miser help us?"

Bob Crachit shook his head. "Mr. Scrooge says he won't help those who can't help themselves." He took Mrs. Crachit's hand in his.

"But Mr. Scrooge's nephew offered to help us."

Tiny Tim's eyes fluttered open. "Mr. Scrooge's nephew will help? Bless him."

"I pray it's not too late," said Mrs. Crachit. "We can't go on without Tiny Tim."

"Without Tiny Tim?" Scrooge gasped. "But that can't be. He's not dying, is he?"

The ghost nodded and turned toward the door. He motioned for Scrooge to follow.

"No!" cried Scrooge. "We can't leave. We must help him. There must be *something* we can do!"

The Crachit's house faded, and Scrooge found himself outside.

Clouds filled the sky, and a wind whipped through the trees. Scrooge glanced around. A gravel path led through rows of granite stones.

"Why, this is a cemetery," said Scrooge. He stared at the ghost. "Oh, no. Not Tiny Tim. Don't tell me you've come here to show me his grave. It can't be too late."

The ghost pointed at a new grave. A priest stood alone, praying. When the prayer was finished, the priest turned and strode away.

"Is this the grave we came to see?" Scrooge frowned. "But where are the Crachits? And the other mourners? Why did no one come to the funeral?"

The ghost motioned toward the headstone. Scrooge squinted. Engraved on a simple stone were two words: EBENEZER SCROOGE.

Scrooge stared. "Mine?" he whispered. "The grave is mine." Scrooge closed his eyes. "I am finally beginning to undertand." He fell to his knees. "Give me another chance. I want to be a different man!"

Scrooge opened his eyes. He was in his own room. From his open window, he spotted a boy on the street. "You! You there!" he shouted. "What day is this?"

"It's Christmas, sir," the boy said.

"Good! Please, lad, do me a favor." Scrooge pulled out a bag of money. He tossed a handful of coins to the boy.

"There's a big, juicy turkey in the butcher shop window at the end of the street. Buy it and deliver it to Bob Crachit's house."

The boy held up the coins. "Sir, this is twice the cost of the turkey."

Scrooge laughed. "Keep the rest for your trouble. Hurry now."

The boy grinned. "Yes, sir!" He scurried away down the street.

Scrooge dressed in his finest clothes, planted his top hat snugly on his head, and set off down the busy, snowy street toward his nephew's house. Everything looked very familiar to Scrooge. "It's just like before," he said, "when the Ghost of Christmas Present showed me the street on Christmas morning."

He tipped his hat to a group of carolers. A family hurried down the street toward the church, and Scrooge stopped to pat their young son on the head.

"Merry Christmas," said Scrooge.

"Merry Christmas to you," said the boy's mother.

When Scrooge reached his nephew's house, his nephew was surprised to see him. "Uncle!" he cried. "Did you change your mind about Christmas dinner? Have you come to celebrate?"

"Yes," said Scrooge. "If you will have me."

"We'd be delighted to have you!" said his nephew.

After dinner, Scrooge said, "Thank you. That was a delicious meal. I hate to leave, but I have another stop to make." He hurried down the street to Bob Crachit's house.

From that day on, each time he sat down to a meal with his friends and family, Scrooge would raise his glass in a toast. "God bless us," he would say. "God bless us every one."

Deck the Halls

Welsh

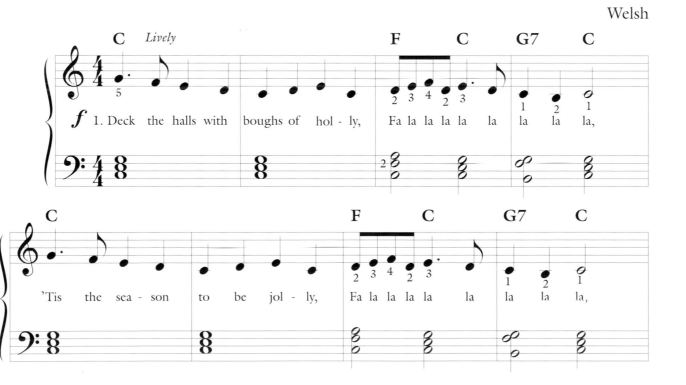

C *Lively*

F   **C**   **G7**   **C**

f 1. Deck the halls with boughs of hol- ly, Fa la la la la   la   la   la   la,

C   **F**   **C**   **G7**   **C**

'Tis the sea- son to be jol- ly, Fa la la la la   la   la   la   la,

2. See the blazing yule before us,
   Fa la la la la la la la la
   Strike the harp and join the chorus,
   Fa la la la la la la la la
   Follow me in merry measure,
   Fa la la la la la la la la
   While I tell of Christmas treasure.
   Fa la la la la la la la la

3. Fast away the old year passes,
   Fa la la la la la la la la
   Hail the New Year, lads and lasses;
   Fa la la la la la la la la
   Sing we joyous all together,
   Fa la la la la la la la la
   Heedless of the wind and weather,
   Fa la la la la la la la la

The Friendly Beasts

Illustrated by Robin Moro

Jesus, our brother, strong and good,
Was humbly born in a stable rude,
And the friendly beasts around Him stood,
Jesus, our brother, strong and good.

"I," said the donkey, shaggy and brown,
"I carried His mother uphill and down,
I carried her safely to Bethlehem town;
I," said the donkey, shaggy and brown.

"I," said the cow, all white and red,
"I gave Him my manger for His bed,
I gave Him my hay to pillow His head;
I," said the cow, all white and red.

"I," said the sheep, with curly horn,
"I gave Him my wool for His blanket warm,
He wore my coat on Christmas morn;
I," said the sheep, with curly horn.

"I," said the dove, from the rafters high,
"Cooed Him to sleep, my mate and I,
We cooed Him to sleep, my mate and I;
I," said the dove, from the rafters high.

And every beast, by some good spell,
In the stable dark was glad to tell,
Of the gift he gave Immanuel,
The gift he gave Immanuel.

O Come, All Ye Faithful

Latin: J. Reading
English translation: Rev. F. Oakeley

Traditional

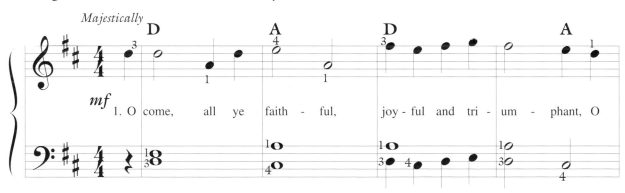

Majestically

D   **A**   **D**   **A**

mf
1. O come, all ye faith - ful, joy - ful and tri - um - phant, O

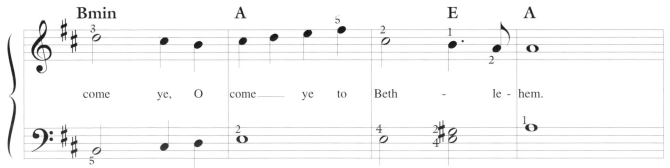

Bmin   **A**   **E**   **A**

come ye, O come ye to Beth - le - hem.

2. Sing, choirs of angels, sing in exultation,
    O Sing, all ye citizens of heav'n above.
    Glory to God, glory in the highest,
    O come, let us adore Him,
    O come, let us adore Him,
    O come, let us adore Him,
    Christ the Lord.

3. Yea Lord, we greet Thee, born this happy morning,
    Jesus, to Thee be glory giv'n.
    Word of the Father, now in flesh appearing.
    O come, let us adore Him,
    O come, let us adore Him,
    O come, let us adore Him,
    Christ the Lord.

The Gift of the Magi

Written by O. Henry   Illustrated by Wendy Edelson

One dollar and eighty-seven cents. That was all. And sixty-seven cents of it was in pennies. Pennies saved one, two, and three at a time by negotiating with the grocer and the vegetable man and the butcher until one's cheeks burned with embarrassment. Three times Della counted it. One dollar and eighty-seven cents. And the next day would be Christmas.

There was clearly nothing to do but flop down on the shabby little couch and howl. So Della did it. She was beginning to believe that life was made up of sobs, sniffles, and smiles, with sniffles predominating.

While the mistress of the home is gradually subsiding from the first stage to the second, take a look at the home. A furnished flat at $8 per week.

In the vestibule below was a letterbox into which no letter would go, and an electric doorbell from which no mortal finger could coax a ring. Also there was a card bearing the name "Mr. James Dillingham Young."

The "Dillingham" had been flung to the breeze during a former period of prosperity when its possessor was being paid $30 per week. Now, when the income was shrunk to $20, though, they were thinking seriously of contracting to a modest and unassuming "D." But whenever Mr. James Dillingham Young came home and reached his flat above he was called "Jim" and greatly hugged by Mrs. James Dillingham Young, already introduced to you as Della. Which is all very good.

Della stood by the window and looked out dully at a gray cat walking near a fence in the gray backyard. Tomorrow would be Christmas Day, and she had only $1.87 with which to buy Jim a present. She had been saving every penny she could for months, with this result. Twenty dollars a week does not go far. Expenses had been greater than she had calculated. Only $1.87 to buy a present for Jim. Many a happy hour she had spent planning for something nice for him, something fine and rare and sterling, something just a little bit near to being worthy of the honor of being owned by Jim.

There was a pier glass between the windows of the room. Perhaps you have seen a pier glass in an $8 flat. A very thin and very agile person may, by observing his reflection in a rapid sequence of mirrored strips, obtain a fairly accurate conception of his looks. Della, being slender, had mastered the art.

Suddenly she whirled from the window and stood before the glass. Her eyes were shining brilliantly, but her face had lost its color within twenty seconds. Rapidly she pulled down her hair and let it fall to its full length.

Now, there were two possessions of the James Dillingham Youngs in which they both took a mighty pride. One was Jim's gold watch that had been his father's and his grandfather's. The other was Della's hair. Had the queen of Sheba lived in the flat across the air shaft, Della would have let her hair hang out the window to dry just to depreciate Her Majesty's jewels and gifts. Had King Solomon been the janitor, with all his treasures piled up in the basement, Jim would have pulled out his watch every time he passed, just to see him pluck at his beard from envy.

So now Della's beautiful hair fell about her, rippling and shining like a cascade of brown waters. It reached below her waist and made itself almost a garment for her. And then she did it up again nervously and quickly.

On went her old brown jacket; on went her old brown hat. With a whirl of skirts and with the sparkle still in her eyes, she fluttered out the door and down the stairs.

Where she stopped the sign read: "Madame Sofronie. Hair Goods of All Kinds." One flight up Della ran, and collected herself, panting. Madame Sofronie was large and chilly. She hardly looked the "Sofronie."

"Will you buy my hair?" asked Della.

"I buy hair," said Madame. "Take yer hat off and let's have a sight at the looks of it."

Down rippled the brown cascade.

"Twenty dollars," said Madame, lifting the mass with a practiced hand.

"Give it to me quick," said Della.

The next two hours tripped by on rosy wings. Della was ransacking the stores for Jim's present.

She found it at last. It surely had been made for Jim and no one else. There was no other like it in any of the stores, and she had turned all of them inside out. It was a platinum fob chain, simple and chaste in design, properly proclaiming its value by substance alone.

As soon as she saw it she knew that it must be Jim's. It was like him. Quietness and value, the description applied to both. Twenty-one dollars they took from her for it, and she hurried home with the eighty-seven cents. With that chain on his watch Jim might be properly anxious about the time in any company. Grand as the watch was, he sometimes looked at it on the sly on account of the old leather strap that he used in place of a chain.

When Della reached home her intoxication gave way a little to prudence and reason. She got out her curling iron and lighted the gas and went to work repairing the ravages made by generosity added to love.

Within forty minutes her head was covered with tiny, close-lying curls that made her look wonderfully like a truant schoolboy. She looked at her reflection in the mirror long, carefully, and critically.

"If Jim doesn't kill me," she said to herself, "before he takes a second look at me, he'll say I look like a Coney Island chorus girl. But what could I do? Oh! What could I do with a dollar and eighty-seven cents?"

At seven o'clock the coffee was made and the frying pan was sitting on the back of the stove.

It was hot and ready to cook the pork chops that Della had bought the night before. Jim was never late. Della doubled the fob chain in her hand and sat on the corner of the table near the door that he always entered. She waited impatiently.

Then Della heard his step on the stairs way down on the first flight. Quickly, she stood up and fixed her hair one last time. Then she turned white for just a moment. Della had a habit of saying little silent prayers about the simplest everyday things, and now she whispered, "Please God, make him think I am still pretty. Make him love me just the same."

The door opened, and Jim stepped in and closed it. He looked thin and very serious. Poor fellow, he was only twenty-two and already burdened with a family! He needed a new overcoat and he was without gloves.

"Hello, dear," Jim said. Then he looked up at Della. Jim stopped inside the door, as immovable as a setter at the scent of quail. His eyes were fixed upon Della as she stood in front of the pier glass.

Della tried to smile, until she looked into his eyes. There was an expression in them that she could not read, and it terrified her. It was not anger, nor surprise, nor disapproval, nor horror, nor any of the sentiments that she had been prepared for. He simply stared at her fixedly with that peculiar expression on his face.

Della finally moved and went for him. "Jim, darling," she cried, "please don't look at me that way. I had my hair cut off and sold because I could not have lived through Christmas without giving you a real present. And I certainly didn't have enough money saved."

Della held Jim's hands and looked into his eyes. "It will grow out again," she said. "You won't mind, will you? I just had to do it. My hair grows awfully fast. Please say 'Merry Christmas!' Jim, and let's be happy."

"You've cut off your hair?" asked Jim, as if he had not arrived at that patent fact yet even after the hardest mental labor.

Della held his hand tighter still, warming it with her own. "Cut it off and sold it," said Della. "Don't you like me just as well, anyhow? I'm me without my hair. Don't you think so?"

Jim looked about the room curiously. "You say your hair is gone?" he said, with an air almost of idiocy.

"You needn't look for it," said Della. "It's sold, I tell you, sold and gone, too. It's Christmas Eve, boy. Be good to me, for it went for you. Maybe the hairs of my head were numbered," she went on with sudden serious sweetness, "but nobody could ever count my love for you." Della waited for Jim to speak then. He took off his coat without speaking and then turned back to Della.

Out of his trance Jim seemed quickly to wake. He grabbed Della in his arms.

For ten seconds let us regard with discreet scrutiny some inconsequential object in the other direction. Eight dollars a week or a million a year, what is the difference? A mathematician would give you the wrong answer. The Magi brought valuable gifts, but that was not among them. This dark assertion will be illuminated later on.

Jim drew a package from his overcoat pocket and threw it upon the table. "Do not make a mistake, Dell, about me," he said. "I don't think there is anything in the way of a haircut or a shave or a shampoo that could make me like my girl any less. But if you will unwrap that small package you may see why you had me going awhile at first."

White, nimble fingers tore at the string and paper. Della let out an ecstatic scream of joy. Then her voice turned to hysterical tears and wails as she examined the contents of the box.

For there lay "the combs," the set of combs, side and back, that Della had worshiped long in a Broadway window. Beautiful combs, pure tortoise shell, with jeweled rims, just the shade to wear in the beautiful vanished hair. They were very expensive combs, she knew, and her heart had simply yearned over them without the least hope of possession. And now, they were hers, but the tresses that should have adorned them were gone.

Jim said, "I can take the combs back and get the money."

But she hugged them to her bosom. "My hair grows so fast, Jim!" she cried.

And then Della leaped up and cried, "Oh, oh!" Jim had not yet seen his beautiful present. She held it out to him eagerly upon her open palm. The dull precious metal seemed to flash with a reflection of her bright and ardent spirit. "Isn't it a dandy, Jim?" Della asked. "I hunted all over town to find it. Give me your watch. I want to see how it looks on it."

Instead of obeying, Jim tumbled down on the couch and put his hands under the back of his head and smiled.

"Dell," said Jim, "let's put our Christmas presents away and keep them awhile. They're too nice to use just yet. I sold the watch to get the money to buy your combs. And now suppose we get dinner ready."

The Magi, as you know, were wise men who brought gifts to the Babe in the manger. They invented the art of giving Christmas presents. And here I have lamely related to you the uneventful chronicle of two foolish children in a flat who most unwisely sacrificed for each other the greatest treasures of their house.

But in a last word to the wise of these days let it be said that of all who give gifts these two were the wisest. Of all who give and receive gifts, they are wisest.

They are the Magi.

God Rest Ye Merry Gentlemen

London

3. The shepherds at those tidings
   Rejoiced much in mind
   And left their flocks a-feeding
   In tempest, storm, and wind,
   And went straightway to Bethlehem
   The Son of God to find.
   O tidings of comfort and joy,
   Comfort and joy,
   O tidings of comfort and joy.

4. And when they came to Bethlehem,
   Where our dear Saviour lay,
   They found Him in a manger
   Where oxen feed on hay;
   His Mother Mary kneeling down
   Unto the Lord did pray.
   O tidings of comfort and joy,
   Comfort and joy,
   O tidings of comfort and joy.

Christmas Greeting From a Fairy to a Child

Written by Lewis Carroll   Illustrated by Marty Noble

Lady, dear, if Fairies may
    For a moment lay aside
Cunning tricks and elfish play,
    'Tis at happy Christmastide.

We have heard the children say,
    Gentle children, whom we love,
Long ago on Christmas Day,
    Came a message from above.

Still as Christmastide comes round,
    They remember it again.
Echo still the joyful sounds
    "Peace on earth, goodwill to men!"

Yet the hearts must childlike be
    Where such heavenly guests abide;
Unto children, in their glee,
    All the year is Christmastide!

Thus, forgetting tricks and play
    For a moment, Lady dear,
We would wish you, if we may,
    Merry Christmas, glad New Year!

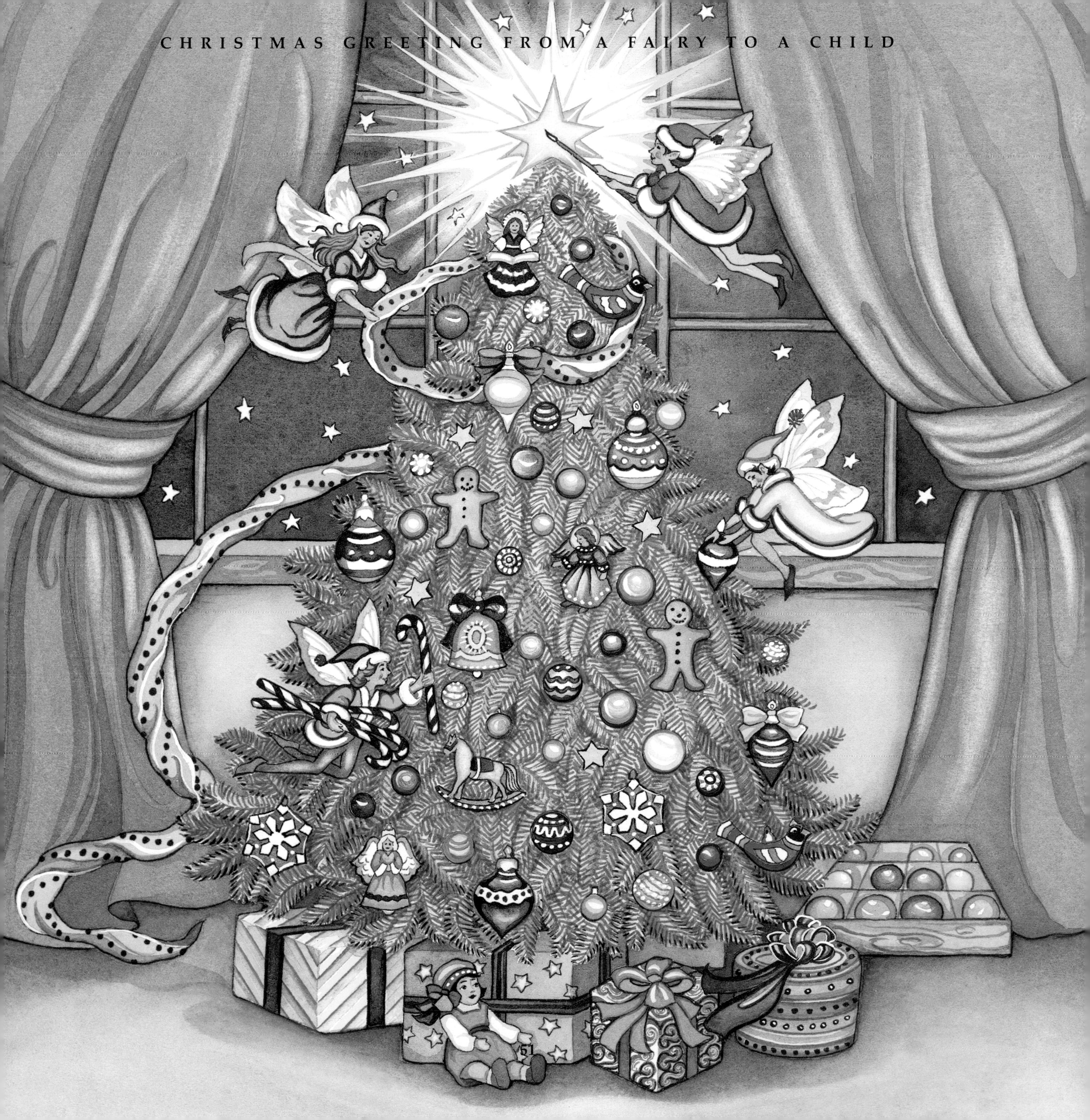

The First Noel

Old English

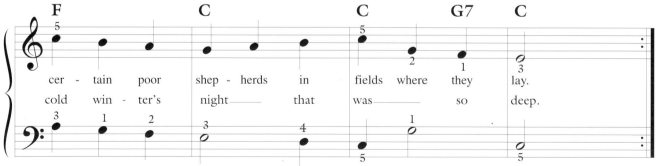

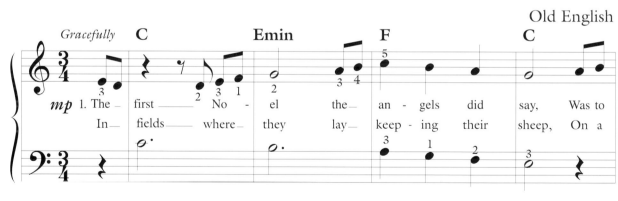

2. They looked up and saw a star
   Shining in the East beyond them far,
   And to the earth it gave great light,
   And so it continued both day and night.
   Noel, Noel, Noel, Noel,
   Born is the King of Israel.

3. This star drew nigh to the northwest,
   O'er Bethlehem it took its rest.
   And there it did both stop and stay
   Right over the place where Jesus lay.
   Noel, Noel, Noel, Noel,
   Born is the King of Israel.

The Nutcracker

Adapted by E.T.A. Hoffman   Illustrated by Linda Dockey Graves

On the twenty-fourth of December, Dr. Stahlbaum's children were not allowed to set foot in the family parlor. Fritz and Clara sat together in the back room and waited. In whispers Fritz told his sister that he had seen Godfather Drosselmeier. At that, Clara clapped her hands for joy and cried out, "Oh, what do you think Godfather Drosselmeier has made for us?"

Fritz said it was a fortress, with all kinds of soldiers marching up and down.

"No, no," Clara interrupted. "Godfather Drosselmeier said something to me about a beautiful garden with a big lake and lovely swans swimming all around."

"Godfather Drosselmeier can't make a whole garden," said Fritz rather rudely.

Then the children tried to guess what their parents would give them. While Clara sat deep in thought, Fritz muttered, "I'd like a chestnut horse and some soldiers."

At that moment, a bell rang, the doors flew open, and a flood of light streamed in from the big parlor. "Come in, dear children," said Papa and Mama.

The children stood silently with shining eyes. Then Clara cried out, "Oh, how lovely! The tree is spectacular!"

Meanwhile, Fritz galloped around the table, trying out the new horse he had found. Then he reviewed his new squadron of soldiers, who were admirably outfitted in red and gold uniforms.

Just then, the bell rang again. Knowing that Godfather Drosselmeier would be unveiling his present, the children ran to the table set up beside the wall. The screen that had hidden it was taken away. The children saw a magnificent castle with dozens of sparkling windows and golden towers.

Chimes played as tiny ladies and gentlemen strolled around the rooms, and children in little skirts danced to the music.

Fritz looked at the beautiful castle, then said, "Godfather Drosselmeier, let me go inside your castle."

"Impossible," said Godfather Drosselmeier.

"Then make the children come out," cried Fritz.

"No," said their godfather crossly, "that, too, is impossible. This is how the mechanism works, and it cannot be changed."

"Then I don't really care for it," said Fritz. "My soldiers march as I command and they're not shut up in a house." Fritz marched away to play with his soldiers.

Clara did not leave the Christmas table, for she was well-behaved. The real reason Clara did not want to leave the Christmas table was that she had just caught sight of something.

When Fritz marched away, an excellent little man came into view. The distinction of his dress showed him to be a man of taste and breeding. Oddly enough, he wore a skimpy cloak that was made of wood. His green eyes were full of kindness and his cotton beard was most becoming.

"Oh, Father," Clara cried out, "who does the little man belong to?"

"Dear child," said Dr. Stahlbaum, "our friend here will serve you well. He will crack hard nuts for you with his teeth."

Carefully picking him up from the table, Dr. Stahlbaum lifted his wooden cloak, and the little man opened his mouth wide, revealing two rows of sharp white teeth. At her father's bidding, Clara put in a nut, and—crack—the little man bit it in two. The shell fell down and Clara found the sweet kernel in her hand.

Fritz ran over to his sister. He chose the biggest nut, and all of a sudden—crack, crack—three little teeth fell out of the Nutcracker's mouth.

"Oh, my poor little Nutcracker!" Clara cried, taking him out of Fritz's hands.

"He's just a fool," said Fritz. "He calls himself a nutcracker, but his teeth are no good. Give him to me, Clara."

Clara was in tears. "No, no!" she cried. "He's my Nutcracker and you can't have him." Sobbing, Clara wrapped the Nutcracker in her handkerchief. She bandaged his wounded mouth. Then she rocked him in her arms like a baby.

It was getting late and Mother urged her children to turn in for the night. But Clara pleaded, "Just a little while longer, Mother."

Clara's mother put out all of the candles, leaving on only one lamp. "Go to bed soon," she said, "or you won't be able to get up tomorrow."

"Thank you," Clara said smiling.

As soon as Clara was alone, she set the Nutcracker carefully on the table, unwrapped the handkerchief ever so slowly, and examined his wounds.

"Nutcracker," she said softly, "don't be angry at my brother Fritz. He meant no harm. I'm going to take care of you until you're well and happy again."

Clara picked up the Nutcracker and placed him next to the other toys in a cabinet in the parlor. She was going to her bedroom when she heard whispering and shuffling. The clock whirred twelve times. Then she heard giggling and squeaking all around her, followed by the sound of a thousand tiny feet scampering behind the walls. Soon Clara saw mice all over the room. Noisily they formed ranks, just as Fritz's soldiers did.

Crushed stone flew out of the floor as though driven by some underground force, and seven mouse heads with seven sparkling crowns rose up, squeaking and squealing hideously.

58

This enormous mouse, with seven heads, was hailed by the entire army, cheering with three loud squeaks. And then the army set itself in motion—hop, hop, trot, trot—heading straight for the toy cabinet.

At the same time, Clara saw a strange glow inside the toy cabinet. All at once, the Nutcracker jumped from the cabinet, and the squeaking and squealing started again.

"Trusty Vassal-Drummer," cried the Nutcracker, "sound the advance!" The drummer played so loudly that the windows of the toy cabinet rattled. A clattering was heard from inside and all the boxes containing Fritz's army burst open. Soldiers climbed out and jumped to the bottom shelf. Then they formed ranks on the floor. The Nutcracker ran back and forth, shouting words of encouragement to the troops.

A few moments later, guns roared boom! boom! The mice advanced and overran some of the artillery positions. Such was the confusion, and such were the smoke and dust, that Clara could hardly see what was happening. But this much was certain—both sides fought with grim determination, and for a long while victory hung in the balance. Then the mice brought up more troops.

The Nutcracker found himself trapped against the toy cabinet. "Bring up the reserves!" he cried. And sure enough, a few men came out, but they wielded their swords so clumsily that they knocked off General Nutcracker's cap.

The Nutcracker was in dire peril. He tried to jump over the ledge of the cabinet, but his legs were too short. In despair he shouted, "A horse, a horse! My kingdom for a horse!"

At that moment, the Mouse King charged the Nutcracker. Without quite knowing what she was doing, Clara took off her left shoe and flung it with all her might, hoping to hit the Mouse King. Then, everything vanished from Clara's sight. She felt a sharp pain in her left arm and fell to the floor.

When Clara awoke from her deep sleep, she was lying in her own little bed. The sun shining into the room sparkled on the ice-coated windowpanes. A strange gentleman was sitting beside her, but she soon recognized him as Dr. Wendelstern. "She's awake," he said softly to Clara's mother. She came over and gave Clara an anxious look.

"Oh, Mother dear," Clara whispered. "Have all the nasty mice gone away? Was the Nutcracker saved?"

Clara's mother sighed. "What have mice got to do with the Nutcracker? Oh, we've been very worried about you. Last night, I found you lying beside the toy cabinet in a faint, bleeding terribly..."

"Oh, Mother," Clara broke in. "There had just been a big battle between the toy soldiers and the mice. The mice were going to capture the poor Nutcracker. I threw my shoe at the mice, and after that I don't know what happened."

Clara's father and mother had a long talk with Dr. Wendelstern. Clara had to stay in bed and take medicine for a week.

When Godfather Drosselmeier came to visit, he brought books and lovely sweets of every color. "I've brought you something else that will give you pleasure," he told Clara. With that, he reached into his pocket and took out the Nutcracker, whose lost teeth had been put back in very neatly and firmly, and whose broken jaw had been fixed as good as new. Clara cried out for joy!

That night, Clara was awakened in the moonlight by the strange rumbling of a thousand tiny feet. "Oh, the mice are here again!" Clara cried out in fright.

Then she saw the Mouse King squeeze through a hole in the wall. He scurried across the floor and jumped onto the table beside Clara's bed. "Give me your candy," he said, "or I'll bite your Nutcracker to pieces." Then he slipped back into the hole.

Clara was so frightened that she could hardly say a word. That night she put her whole supply of delicacies at the foot of her bed. By morning, every last piece of the colorful candy was gone. Clara was happy because she had saved the Nutcracker.

That night, however, the Mouse King returned. "Give me your most beautiful dress and all your picture books," he hissed.

Clara was beside herself with anguish.

The next morning she went to the toy cabinet sobbing and said to the Nutcracker, "Oh, what can I do? If I give that horrid Mouse King all my books and my dress, he'll just keep asking for more."

The Nutcracker said in a strained whisper, "Find me a sword." At that his words ebbed away, and his eyes became fixed.

Clara asked Fritz for a sword, and Fritz slung it around the Nutcracker's waist.

The next night fear and dread kept Clara awake. At the stroke of twelve she heard clanging and crashing in the parlor. And then suddenly, "Squeak!"

Soon Clara heard a soft knocking at the door and a faint little voice say, "Miss Stahlbaum, open the door and have no fear. I bring good news!"

Clara swiftly opened the door and found that the Nutcracker had turned into a prince!

The prince took Clara's hand and told her how he was really Godfather Drosselmeier's nephew, and an evil spell had turned him into a nutcracker. When he defeated the Mouse King, the spell was broken and he was turned back into a prince.

"Oh, Miss Stahlbaum," said the prince, "what splendid things I can show you in this hour of victory over my enemy, if you will follow me a little way."

Clara agreed and followed the prince to the big clothes cupboard in the entrance hall. The door of the cupboard was wide open.

The prince stepped inside, pulled a tassel, and a little ladder came down through the sleeve of a traveling coat. Clara climbed the ladder and soon passed through the sleeve.

When Clara looked out through the neck hole, she found herself in a fragrant meadow.

"This is Candy Meadow," said the prince.

Looking up, Clara saw a beautiful arch as they were passing through it. "Oh, it's so wonderful here," she sighed.

The prince clapped his hands, and a little shepherd appeared. He brought up a golden chair and asked Clara to sit down. Then the young shepherd danced a charming ballet. Suddenly, as if at a signal, he vanished into the woods.

The prince took Clara's hand and led her on a tour of his kingdom. They walked through Gingerbread Grove, where icing lined the rooftops of each charming house. They strolled along a beautiful stream, where plump red fruit grew taller than the two of them. They walked across bridges and had a lovely picnic in the Frosted Forest.

In the distance Clara saw a beautiful city with a giant castle. "I have never seen anything so fantastic!" Clara exclaimed. "Can we go there?"

"Clap three times," said the prince.

Clara laughed and clapped three times.

Suddenly, a gondola appeared. Clara and the prince stepped onto the gondola and were gently whisked away toward the distant city.

Not only were the walls and towers the most magnificent colors, but the shapes of the buildings were like nothing else on earth.

Suddenly, Clara saw a castle with a hundred lofty towers. "This," said the prince, "is Marzipan Castle." At that moment they heard soft music. The gates of the castle opened, and out stepped four ladies so richly and splendidly attired that Clara knew they could only be princesses. One by one, they embraced their brother.

The ladies led Clara and the prince to an inner room with walls made of sparkling colored crystal. The princesses prepared a meal for Clara and the prince. They brought in the most wonderful fruit and candy Clara had ever seen and began to squeeze the fruit and grate the sugared almonds.

The most beautiful of the prince's sisters handed her a little golden mortar and said, "Dear sweet friend, would you care to pound some rock candy?"

While Clara pounded away, the prince told the history of the cruel war between the Mouse King's army and his own.

As Clara listened to his story, she began to feel very dizzy. The room began to spin and Clara felt as though she were falling.

Clara fell to the floor. When she opened her eyes, she was lying in her little bed, and her mother was standing there.

"Clara, how in the world can anyone sleep so long!" her mother exclaimed.

"Oh, Mother," said Clara, "you cannot imagine all of the places that young Mr. Drosselmeier took me to last night."

Clara's mother looked at her in disbelief. "You've had a long, beautiful dream," she said.

"But, Mother," said Clara, "the Nutcracker is really young Mr. Drosselmeier, Godfather Drosselmeier's nephew." Mrs. Stahlbaum burst out laughing. "You're to forget about this foolishness once and for all." So Clara did.

One day Clara's mother entered her room and said, "Your godfather's nephew from Nuremberg is here. So be on your best behavior."

Clara turned as red as a beet when she saw the young man, and she turned even redder when young Drosselmeier asked her to go with him to the cabinet in the parlor. He went down on one knee and said, "Miss Stahlbaum, you see at your feet the happiest of young men, whose life you saved on this very spot. Please promise me that one day you will come and reign with me over Marzipan Castle."

Clara said softly, "Of course I will come with you."

Years later, Clara left in a golden carriage. She is still the queen of a country where the most wonderful things can be seen if you have the right sort of eyes for it.

Dance of the Sugarplum Fairy

Rhythmically and Delicately
2nd time play both hands one octave higher

Tchaikovsky
from *The Nutcracker Suite*

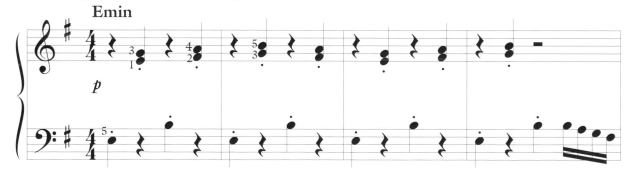

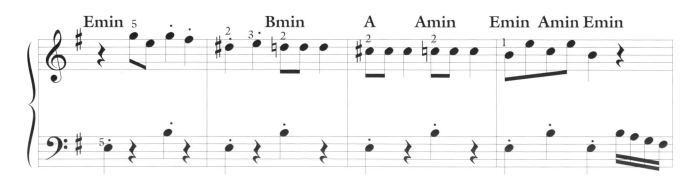

Yes, Virginia, There Is a Santa Claus

Written by Francis P. Church   *Illustrated by Janet Wilson*

Editorial Page, *New York Sun,* **1897**

We take pleasure in answering thus prominently the communication below, expressing at the same time our great gratification that its faithful author is numbered among the friends of *The Sun:*

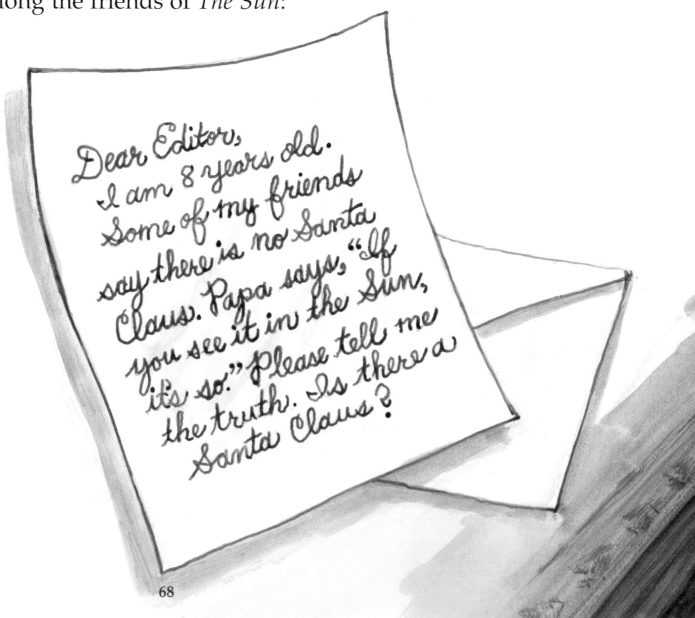

Dear Editor,
I am 8 years old.
Some of my friends
say there is no Santa
Claus. Papa says, "If
you see it in the Sun,
it's so." Please tell me
the truth. Is there a
Santa Claus?

Virginia, your little friends are wrong. They do not believe except what they see.

Yes, Virginia, there is a Santa Claus. He exists as certainly as love and generosity and devotion exist, and you know that they abound and give to your life its highest beauty and joy. Alas! How dreary would be the world if there were no Santa Claus! It would be as dreary as if there were no Virginias. There would be no childlike faith then, no poetry, no romance to make tolerable this existence. We should have no enjoyment, except in sense and sight. The external light with which childhood fills the world would be extinguished.

Not believe in Santa Claus! You might as well not believe in fairies. You might get your papa to hire men to watch in all the chimneys on Christmas Eve to catch Santa Claus, but even if you did not see Santa Claus coming down, what would that prove? Nobody sees Santa Claus, but that is no sign that there is no Santa Claus. The most real things in the world are those that neither children nor men can see. Did you ever see fairies dancing on the lawn? Of course not, but that's no proof that they are not there. Nobody can conceive or imagine all the wonders that are unseen and unseeable in the world.

You tear apart the baby's rattle and see what makes the noise inside, but there is a veil covering the unseen world which not the strongest man, nor even the united strength of all the strongest men that ever lived could tear apart. Only faith, poetry, love, romance, can push aside that curtain and view and picture the supernal beauty and glory beyond. Is it all real? Ah, Virginia, in all this world there is nothing as real and abiding.

No Santa Claus? Thank God he lives and lives forever. A thousand years from now, Virginia, nay 10 times 10,000 years from now, he will continue to make glad the heart of childhood.

We Wish You a Merry Christmas

Traditional

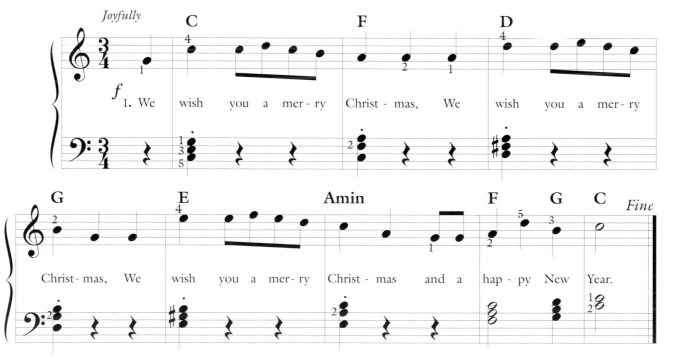

2. Now bring us some figgy pudding,
   Now bring us some figgy pudding,
   Now bring us some figgy pudding
   And a cup of good cheer!

3. We won't go until we get some,
   We won't go until we get some,
   We won't go until we get some,
   So bring it out here.

The Tailor's Apprentices

Written by Leslie Lindecker Illustrated by Mike Jaroszko

Back in the days when men wore beautiful clothes and wigs, there was a very poor tailor. He worked diligently and spent all of his money on lovely fabrics. He worked from dawn to the last light of dusk, making beautiful garments for the citizens of the town. Although his own coat was quite threadbare and popping at the seams, the coats and vests he made for the townsfolk were fine silk and satin, warm velvet and corduroy.

As he snipped and stitched, the tailor hummed a tune and talked to the mice who lived beneath the floor. A little mouse hopped up onto the end of the tailor's worktable. The tailor smiled and said, "Someday, my friend, my hard work will be rewarded. Until then, you must appreciate the snips and threads, bits and ends which are too small for me to use. These are barely big enough to make hats and vests for you."

The mouse winked at the tailor, then daintily picked up a bit of ribbon from the table, scrambled to the floor, and disappeared into the woodwork. The tailor laughed softly to himself and continued to sew.

On the very day the good mayor of the town announced his wedding was to be on Christmas Day, the tailor received a request from the mayor for a special new suit.

74

The tailor danced with glee. The mice poked their long noses out from under his worktable to see what was happening.

"My little friends," the tailor said, "you shall have the finest bits of lace and thread, because I am going to make the mayor's suit for his wedding on Christmas Day! It shall be of my best emerald satin, embroidered and stitched with gold. I shall make a beautiful vest also, all trimmed with lace. A happy day, indeed!" The mice squealed in agreement and scurried out from under the tailor's dancing feet.

The tailor measured and marked, and measured again. He cut out the coat from the emerald cloth with shears and trimmed it carefully with small snips. He spun the cloth around and measured once again.

"No waste on this fabric. Just enough for a suit for a mouse, and such a grand suit that would be, all stitched with gold!" the tailor said.

Soon, the table was covered with cut pieces of coat atop more pieces for the vest. There were buttons and bows, flaps for the pockets and cuffs for the sleeves. The floor was littered with bits of green and gold thread and lace. Everything was ready to begin sewing the beautiful emerald suit in the morning, except for one spool of thread.

The tailor heaved a sigh, took off his spectacles, and rubbed his eyes. "We will begin again in the morning, my friends. It is too dark to sew tonight."

The tailor pulled on his old, worn-out coat, snuffed the candle, and stepped out of his shop into the snowy December night. He fastened the window latch and locked the door, putting the key into his pocket. He shuffled through the snow and up the rickety stairs to the room he rented above his shop.

The tailor lived alone with his cat, whom he called Tomkin. As he unlocked the door, Tomkin meowed. "Tomkin, old friend," said the tailor, "fortune has finally smiled upon us, but I am worn out beyond working this night."

The tailor built up the fire in the grate, then took a scrap of paper and made a list. "Tomkin, old friend, I need you to go to the shopkeeper. We need a bottle of milk, a bit of bread, and I must have a spool of golden thread for the mayor's new suit. Please don't forget the golden thread." He tied the list and his last dollar to Tomkin's collar, then opened the door for the cat.

Tomkin walked slowly into the cold night. Although he was usually a faithful cat, Tomkin wasn't fond of the cold. In fact, he hated the cold.

Instead of milk, bread, and a spool of golden thread, Tomkin had mice on his mind. Tomkin spent much of his time chasing the fast, crafty mice. They were often too fast for him. He would run and pounce at them, but they would slip away under the floorboards.

That day, Tomkin was especially fortunate. He had caught many mice that morning. Saving them for his supper, Tomkin trapped the small mice under bowls and cups. At least after his long walk in the cold, he would enjoy a fine meal.

The tailor was very tired. "I fear I've a touch of the flu," he said as he felt his forehead. He went to bed and talked to himself about the mayor's new suit. Feverish, the tailor reached out to touch the beautiful emerald fabric and the crisp, white lace. He imagined the most beautiful suit.

"The mayor will be pleased when he wears this fine suit," he said to himself. "The finest suit, fit for a mayor on Christmas Day."

Suddenly the tailor heard a tip-tip-tap coming from somewhere in the small room. It was the faintest of tip-tip-taps, and he was weak with fever, but still he went to investigate. He searched under the bed. He searched under the sink. He searched under the rug. He searched under the table. He could see nothing, but he continued to hear the tip-tip-tapping. The sound was the loudest at the side of the sink.

At the sink, his teacups and mugs, bowls and pots were all turned upside down. From under one of the teacups he heard the tip-tip-tap again.

Slowly the tailor lifted the teacup, and out popped a lovely lady mouse. She smiled, wiggled her long brown nose at him, and scampered away. The tailor took off his spectacles and rubbed his eyes. Then he heard a scritch-scritch-scratch. He looked under a bowl and was met with the gaze of a handsome gentleman mouse, who bowed to the tailor before running away.

"I truly must be ill, for I swear that mouse was wearing a hat!" exclaimed the tailor. "I do believe my dear old Tomkin has been very busy, and I don't think he captured these mice for company!" The tailor began to turn over all the teacups and mugs, bowls and pots to find many little mice hopping and bobbing and running about.

The tailor continued to talk to himself as he prepared for bed. "Was it right to free those mice, who should have been kept for Tomkin? What shall I do without that spool of golden thread? Ah, the mayor's suit shall be my finest creation. But can I finish it by Christmas Day?"

The little mice listened to the tailor as he muttered on about the suit for the mayor. All at once, they began to squeak and scamper, then they all ran away.

Tomkin nudged open the door and walked in with a gust of cold air. He hated snow, and it was in his ears and under his collar. He jumped up on the table and dropped the sack he carried in his mouth containing the bottle of milk and the bit of bread.

Then Tomkin spied the overturned teacups and upturned bowls. With an angry cat snarl, he jumped onto the sink, swatting a cup to the floor in search of the fat little mice he was saving for dinner.

"Tomkin, old friend," the tailor said from his bed. "It is late and I am not well. Did you get my spool of golden thread?"

Being in an ill-tempered mood, Tomkin hid the spool of thread under the teapot lid. He jumped up onto the tailor's bed and kneaded the quilt with his claws.

Tomkin jumped to the floor as the
tailor dozed, hunting throughout the room
for even one of the mice he had captured. Tomkin
looked behind doors, into cabinets, and under the bed,
but not one mouse was to be found. The two of them made
a strange chorus that night with the tailor feverishly muttering
about his golden thread, accompanied by Tomkin meowing and
growling for his little lost mice.

The tailor was indeed sick and remained in bed for several days, tossing and
turning with fever. He mumbled about the mayor's new suit and cried about his need
for a spool of golden thread.

Christmas Day was fast approaching, and he was too ill to work. Tomkin mewed for
the little brown mice that were lost, and he fed on the bit of bread and the bottle of milk
he had fetched a few days before. How he wanted those mice!

Christmas Eve came and the good folk of the town scurried about on their rounds in
preparation for Christmas Day. No one thought at all of the tailor's tiny shop and the
fine suit of clothes for the mayor, that lay upon the table.

Later that night as the old cathedral bells rang out the midnight hour, the animals in the town lifted their voices to celebrate the coming of Christmas Day. A great cat and dog chorus commenced, while birds in the eaves sang praises. However, Tomkin's attention was most drawn to the voices coming from inside the tailor's small shop.

Tomkin heard this great noise, and he went down the rickety steps and into the snow to find out what was happening. From the window ledge he peeked into the shop. In the candlelight, Tomkin could see his little brown mice, the very same ones the tailor had let go, singing and dancing—and sewing! They were stitching the beautiful emerald coat with the golden thread. They sang as they applied the lace to the wonderful vest. And they danced about in the mouse hats and mouse vests they had made from the scraps and threads, bits and ribbon ends the tailor had left for them.

Tomkin yowled through the window at the mice. They jumped, startled at the sound, then giggled and waved at the cat who was peeking through the glass. They continued to sew and to dance to their songs, keeping time with the click of their thimbles and whisk of their needles. Tomkin tried to pull the latch on the door, but the key was safely in the pocket of the tailor's old coat, and he couldn't get in.

Fascinated, he watched the little mice sew the mayor's new suit. Near dawn, he heard the mice cry in chorus, "No more golden thread!"

He peered in through the window to see the mice scampering away through the woodwork of the shop. Tomkin jumped down from the window ledge and went up the steps to the tailor's tiny room. There he found the tailor sleeping peacefully.

The cat fetched the spool of golden thread from the teapot and placed it upon the tailor's quilt. Feeling ashamed of his ill temper, Tomkin curled up beside the tailor and nuzzled him awake.

"Tomkin, old friend! You did get my thread," said the tailor. He jumped up from bed and hurried into his old coat. "It's Christmas Day, and what will the mayor do for his suit? I am undone!" he cried.

The tailor hurried down the steps to the shop. He unlocked the door and threw it open. Not one mouse was to be seen, but the tailor gave a shout of joy, for there on the table where he'd left the pieces of satin and silk was the loveliest emerald wedding suit anyone had ever seen. It was stitched with gold, trimmed with buttons and bows, and the vest trimmed with lace. Everything was finished except for one buttonhole. There was a scrap of paper pinned to the buttonhole, reading "NO MORE GOLDEN THREAD," in tiny writing. The tailor danced about the shop, then finished the buttonhole with the thread Tomkin had bought.

Thus began the long and good fortune of the tailor, who grew quite rich, and Tomkin, who grew quite fat.

While Shepherds Watched Their Flocks

George Frederick Handel

1. While shep - herds watched their flocks by night, All seat - ed on the

ground, The an - gel of the Lord came down, And

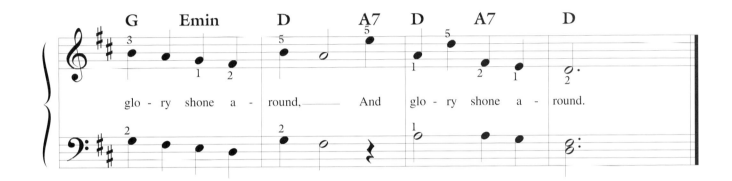

glo - ry shone a - round,———— And glo - ry shone a - round.

2. "Fear not," said he; for mighty dread
   Had seized their trouble mind;
   "Glad tidings of great joy I bring
   To you and all mankind."

3. "To you in David's town this day
   Is born of David's line
   A Saviour, who is Christ the Lord;
   And this shall be the sign."

4. "The heavenly Babe you there shall find
   To human view displayed,
   All meanly wrapped in swathing bands,
   And in a manger laid."

5. Thus spake the seraph; and forthwith
   Appeared a shining throng
   Of angels praising God, who thus
   Addressed their joyful song.

I Am the Christmas Spirit

Written by E. C. Baird

I am the Christmas Spirit!
   I cause the aged to renew their youth,
and to laugh in the old, gay way.
   I keep romance alive in the heart of
childhood, and brighten sleep with
   dreams of woven magic.

I cause eager feet to climb dark
   stairways with filled baskets,
leaving behind hearts amazed at the
   goodness of the world.

Away in a Manger

Old Lutheran Carol

Slowly, Tenderly

1. A - way in a man - ger, no crib for a bed, The

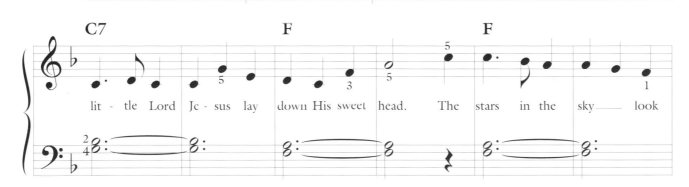

lit - tle Lord Je - sus lay down His sweet head. The stars in the sky look

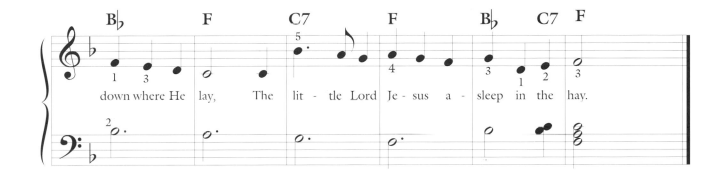

down where He lay, The lit - tle Lord Je - sus a - sleep in the hay.

2. The cattle are lowing, the Baby awakes
   But little Lord Jesus, no crying He makes.
   I love Thee, Lord Jesus, look down from the sky,
   And stay by my cradle 'til morning is nigh.

3. Be near me, Lord Jesus, I ask Thee to stay
   Close by me forever, and love me, I pray.
   Bless all the dear children in Thy tender care,
   And fit us for Heaven to live with Thee there.

The Twelve Days of Christmas

Illustrated by Gwen Connelly

On the first day of Christmas,
My true love sent to me,
A partridge in a pear tree.

On the second day of Christmas,
My true love sent to me,
Two turtle doves,
and a partridge in a pear tree.

On the third day of Christmas,
My true love sent to me,
Three French hens,
Two turtle doves,
and a partridge in a
pear tree.

On the fourth day of Christmas,
My true love sent to me,
Four calling birds,
Three French hens,
Two turtle doves,
and a partridge in a pear tree.

On the fifth day of Christmas,
My true love sent to me,
Five golden rings.
Four calling birds,
Three French hens,
Two turtle doves,
and a partridge in a pear tree.

On the sixth day of Christmas,
  My true love sent to me,
Six geese a-laying,
   Five golden rings.
Four calling birds,
  Three French hens,
Two turtle doves,
  and a partridge in a pear tree.

On the seventh day of Christmas,
  My true love sent to me,
Seven swans a-swimming,
  Six geese a-laying,
Five golden rings.
  Four calling birds,
Three French hens,
  Two turtle doves,
and a partridge in a pear tree.

On the eighth day of Christmas,
My true love sent to me,
Eight maids a-milking,
Seven swans a-swimming,
Six geese a-laying,
Five golden rings.
Four calling birds,
Three French hens,
Two turtle doves,
and a partridge in a pear tree.

On the ninth day of Christmas,
My true love sent to me,
Nine ladies dancing,
Eight maids a-milking,
Seven swans a-swimming,
Six geese a-laying,
Five golden rings.
Four calling birds,
Three French hens,
Two turtle doves,
and a partridge in a pear tree.

On the tenth day of Christmas,
    My true love sent to me,
Ten lords a leaping,
    Nine ladies dancing
Eight maids a-milking,
    Seven swans a-swimming,
Six geese a-laying,
    Five golden rings.
Four calling birds,
    Three French hens,
Two turtle doves,
    and a partridge in a pear tree.

On the eleventh day of Christmas,
    My true love sent to me,
Eleven pipers piping,
    Ten lords a-leaping,
Nine ladies dancing,
    Eight maids a-milking,
Seven swans a-swimming,
    Six geese a-laying,
Five golden rings.
    Four calling birds,
Three French hens,
    Two turtle doves,
        and a partridge in a pear tree.

On the twelfth day of Christmas,
My true love sent to me,
Twelve drummers drumming,
Eleven pipers piping,
Ten lords a-leaping,
Nine ladies dancing,
Eight maids a-milking,
Seven swans a-swimming,
Six geese a-laying,
Five golden rings.
Four calling birds,
Three French hens,
Two turtle doves,
and a partridge in a pear tree.

Hark! The Herald Angels Sing

Words: Charles Wesley

Music: Felix Mendelssohn

1. Hark! The her - ald an - gels sing, Glo - ry to the new - born King,

Peace on earth and mer - cy mild, God and sin - ners re - con - ciled.

2. Christ by highest heav'n adored,
   Christ the everlasting Lord!
   Late in time behold Him come,
   Offspring of a virgin's womb.
   Veiled in flesh the Godhead see,
   Hail the Incarnate Deity,
   Pleased with men as man to dwell,
   Jesus our Immanuel!
   Hark! The herald angels sing
   Glory to the newborn King.

3. Hail, the heav'n-born Prince of Peace!
   Hail, the Son of Righteousness!
   Life and light to all He brings,
   Ris'n with healing in His wings.
   Mild He lays His glory by,
   Born that man no more may die,
   Born to raise the sons of earth,
   Born to give them second birth.
   Hark! The herald angels sing
   Glory to the newborn King.

The End